LEADERSHIP
BRAND

DELIVER ON YOUR PROMISE

IDEAS INTO ACTION SERIES

This series of books draws on the practical knowledge that the Center for Creative Leadership (CCL®) has generated, since its inception in 1970, through its research and educational activity conducted in partnership with hundreds of thousands of managers and executives. Much of this knowledge is shared—in a way that is distinct from the typical university department, professional association, or consultancy. CCL is not simply a collection of individual experts, although the individual credentials of its staff are impressive; rather it is a community, with its members holding certain principles in common and working together to understand and generate practical responses to today's leadership and organizational challenges.

The purpose of the series is to provide managers with specific advice on how to complete a developmental task or solve a leadership challenge. In doing that, the series carries out CCL's mission to advance the understanding, practice, and development of leadership for the benefit of society worldwide. We think you will find the Ideas Into Action Series an important addition to your leadership toolkit.

IDEAS
INTO
ACTION

LEADERSHIP
BRAND

DELIVER ON YOUR PROMISE

David Magellan Horth
Lynn B. Miller
Portia R. Mount

Center for
Creative
Leadership·

IDEAS INTO ACTION SERIES

Aimed at managers and executives who are concerned with their own and others' development, each book in this series gives specific advice on how to complete a developmental task or solve a leadership problem.

LEAD CONTRIBUTORS
David Magellan Horth, Lynn B. Miller, Portia R. Mount

CONTRIBUTORS
Jessica Glazer, Cynthia McCauley

DIRECTOR, PEOPLE, PROCESS, AND PROJECTS
Davida Sharpe

MANAGER, PUBLICATION DEVELOPMENT
Peter Scisco

EDITOR
Stephen Rush

ASSOCIATE EDITOR
Shaun Martin

WRITER
Linda Edgerton

DESIGN, LAYOUT, AND COVER DESIGN
Ed Morgan, navybluedesign.com

RIGHTS AND PERMISSIONS
Kelly Lombardino

EDITORIAL BOARD
David Altman, Elaine Biech, Regina Eckert, Joan Gurvis, Jennifer Habig, Kevin Liu, Neal Maillet, Jennifer Martineau, Portia Mount, Laura Santana

CCL No. 00467

978-1-60491-629-4 – Print
978-1-60491-630-0 – Ebook

Center for Creative Leadership
www.ccl.org

CONTENTS

What is a Leadership Brand?

You have a reputation, whether you deliberately spend time crafting one or not. It is the total of your past experiences and interactions with others. For instance, based on your previous experiences with your team or company, you may have the reputation of a hard worker, a reliable team player, or a go-getter. However, while your reputation is about your past, your brand is about who you are now and who you want to be in the future. It is crafted in the present, aspirational (who am I now, who do I want to become, and how can I get there?), and it can enhance or impede your effectiveness in all aspects of your life. In short, your reputation is what you were to others in the past, while your brand is the promise you make to others in the present.

Your *leadership* brand is how your brand plays out in the social process of leadership. Think about it. Every day is a performance review, as those around you evaluate what you say, what you do, and what you deliver.

As a result, consciously and authentically shaping your leadership brand through your actions and intentions is extremely beneficial. It can help whether you aspire to a higher-level position or just want to be more effective in your current role.

An authentic brand that reflects your most deeply held values can create clarity for you and others about your approach to leadership and the anticipated value you bring to the job. It can influence the effectiveness of your working relationships and can help you become more respected and appreciated for your leadership contributions.

Many people, though, have never thought about their leadership brand. If this includes you, we hope this book inspires you to both pay attention to your current brand and to begin to proactively develop the leadership brand you aspire to.

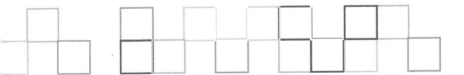

Why Your Brand Matters

A powerful leadership brand can enhance your ability to achieve your career goals and help you build and sustain partnerships that get things done. What's more, your leadership brand can help you broaden and deepen your impact.

One example: Television host Oprah Winfrey has a strong leadership brand that reflects what she describes as her mission: "…to be a teacher…and to be known for inspiring my students to be more than they thought they could be."

Oprah Winfrey has used her fame to promote causes and issues she cares about most, exposing her millions of followers to spiritual leaders, authors, thinkers, and healers who challenge conventional wisdom. So powerful is her influence that it has been dubbed "The Oprah Effect"—reflecting her ability to persuade millions of viewers to buy the books and products she loves.

Though few of us can aspire to Winfrey's fame, we all have our own personal leadership brands. In its optimal state, our brand reflects what matters to us most, the values we stand for, the offerings or promises we consistently deliver, and how we go about delivering them.

Our brand also differentiates us from other leaders based on our own unique value. People know what to expect from us versus others on the team, whether it's organizing complex projects, mediating disagreements, providing subject-matter expertise, being resilient during times of upheaval, or making other contributions. We each bring unique talents to our work, and when people think about our brand, those talents should immediately come to mind.

Without a clear and well-communicated leadership brand, others may be unaware of your capabilities, your value, and the contributions you make. You may end up working in a vacuum, unseen and unheard by your boss, key stakeholders, and even your peers. Promotions and interesting assignments are likely to pass you by, and you could end up derailing your career.

The Link between Brand and the Social Aspects of Leadership

At its core, leadership is a social process that enables individuals to work together as a cohesive group to produce collective results. This process focuses on achieving shared direction, alignment, and commitment among team members.

- WITH DIRECTION, the group is in agreement on overarching goals. Members have a shared understanding of what group success looks like and agree on what they are aiming to accomplish.

- WITH ALIGNMENT, work within the group is well coordinated. Members with different tasks or roles or with different sets of expertise integrate their work instead of working in isolation.

- WITH COMMITMENT, group members put the team's best interests ahead of their own individual interests. They feel responsible for the success and well-being of their team and know others feel the same way. They trust one another and stick together through difficult times.

The way you engage in this social process of leadership creates a leadership brand that others will likely remember and talk about. An effective leadership brand helps you and your team achieve these three crucial outcomes of leadership. Furthermore, your brand reflects not only the work you get done, but also how you interact with and relate to others to do so.

How a Leadership Brand Can Work for You—or Against You

Your leadership brand can work to your benefit or to your detriment—influencing your workplace effectiveness and the very arc of your career. It can determine whether you get noticed and for what. Your brand can also make a difference in your ability to accomplish your career aspirations.

Let's look at three case studies that illustrate the power (positive and negative) of a leadership brand.

CASE STUDY 1
Blending into the background.

Sam is known for getting the job done and being easy to work with. He willingly helps other people with work they have been assigned in order to keep a project moving and would like to get assignments that inspire and stretch him creatively. Too often, though, Sam is handed tasks that simply fail to interest him. Others rarely ask for his input in strategic initiatives or in discussions that help shape goals at the start of a project.

Sam hasn't given much thought to his leadership brand. He assumes doing good work is enough to get him noticed and to one day get assignments he will find more engaging. Unfortunately for Sam, no one seems to pay attention to or care about his work.

FOOD for thought

Are you lacking visibility like Sam? What strategies could you use to enhance your leadership brand and to become more broadly known for something you are good at and like to do?

5

CASE STUDY 2
Moving up or moving out?

Giovanni is a middle manager who hopes to become a member of the senior leadership team—and soon. He values intellect, strategic thinking, creativity, problem solving, and getting the job done. He wants to be known for these qualities, but as the old jazz standard written by Oliver and Young goes: "T'ain't what you do, it's the way that you do it."

While Giovanni's brand stands out, he might be surprised at what people think. His colleagues see Giovanni as all about looking good to the boss. Some see him as a bit of a bully because he often interacts by demanding, threatening, or intimidating others. He also implies that he speaks for senior management, whether he does so or not.

Giovanni's voice dominates almost any conversation about project goals. He believes the thinking he has already done and his ability to communicate are all he needs to get support. His team, however, feels intimidated and railroaded.

Those who influence the next steps in Giovanni's career are closely scrutinizing how Giovanni gets work done. Rather than seeing him as ready for the promotion he covets, they suspect his career is derailing.

FOOD for thought

Are your actions clearly aligned with your career goals? Are you as authentic in your personal interactions with peers and direct reports as you are in those with your boss and executive team?

CASE STUDY 3
A rising star.

Danielle has a distinctive and much-respected leadership brand. She values and is known for collaborative problem solving, innovation, customer focus, and a sense of passion and humor. She is an eager learner and brings an infectious energy to projects.

As an individual contributor, however, Danielle avoids the spotlight. She seeks instead to praise and recognize others for their contributions. Danielle is known for the clarity she brings to the work and to even the most complex issues. She seeks input from both stakeholders and team members, and she uses what she hears to shape goals and objectives.

Danielle is not afraid of conflict. When tensions arise, she often takes a stand and asks tough and sometimes unpopular questions. At the same time, she can use her sense of humor to defuse unnecessary conflict and to promote team unity.

Danielle constantly reminds herself of an adage from executive coach and author Marshall Goldsmith: "What got you here won't get you there." Even though her current brand has served her well, she proactively seeks and acts on feedback she receives from others in order to improve her effectiveness.

FOOD for thought

Do you routinely evaluate your leadership impact and how others react to you? How might you gather feedback that could help you grow and evolve? What do you need to keep doing, start doing, or stop doing? Are there mentors, training opportunities, or challenging job assignments that could help you further your leadership development?

As the experiences of Sam, Giovanni, and Danielle illustrate, your leadership brand can have a significant impact on your effectiveness and the progression of your career. It can impact your ability to interact effectively with others and to contribute to the direction, alignment, and commitment of your team. Your brand can determine whether you are noticed, whether you succeed on the job, or whether your career stutters, stalls, and comes to a premature end.

Defining Your Current Leadership Brand

Taking a close look at your current leadership brand can be eye opening. Having self-awareness is fundamental to defining and evaluating your leadership brand. Self-awareness helps you decide what you need to keep doing, start doing, and stop doing in order to establish a brand that reflects what matters most to you.

In the exercises that follow, you will have an opportunity to focus on the components of a leadership brand—first looking at others and then looking at yourself. The goal is for you to gain perspective on your brand and to determine whether it aligns with your values and what you want to be known for.

Exercise 1:
Developing a Brand Perspective

To help you begin to think with a brand perspective, review and assess the three leader profiles below.

LEADER 1: PARKER

- a software engineer with 11 years of experience
- known as an expert designer with a strong background in software/hardware architecture—often sought after to solve tricky technical issues
- a hard worker who is relentlessly focused on results, with little time for the "touchy-feely" side of the job
- has worked on multiple successful projects in the past
- now managing a multimillion-dollar project for the first time that he hopes will be a stepping stone to a promotion
- strengths (based on 360-degree feedback assessment): decisiveness, strategic perspective, risk-taking, political skill, initiative
- development needs (based on 360-degree feedback assessment): leading others, building collaborative relationships, forging cooperation, self-insight, flexibility
- words others use to describe Parker: skillful, intelligent, cold, determined, practical, industrious
- Parker's self-description: ambitious, change agent, born leader, risk taker, team player
- tagline for Parker by Parker: **GET IT DONE!**

Your assessment of Parker:

- What is Parker known for?
- How do you believe Parker delivers value?
- How do you think Parker influences others?
- What would your tagline for Parker be?
- On a scale of 1 to 10—with 1 being "not really" and 10 being "absolutely"—how much would you enjoy working with Parker?

LEADER 2: JAMES
- communication analyst with five years of experience
- manages internal communications for a midsize global organization
- reports to two bosses: communication director and human resources director
- eager to please
- works collaboratively to keep both bosses informed, but worries about making missteps associated with his complex reporting relationship
- carefully weighs all his options before acting
- known as a strong team leader and team player
- strengths (based on 360-degree feedback assessment): building collaborative relationships, forging cooperation, political skill, self-motivation, flexibility
- development needs (based on 360-degree feedback assessment): strategic perspective, decisiveness, risk-taking, initiative, self-development
- words others use to describe James: collaborative, intelligent, warm, determined, politically skillful, flexible
- James's self-description: team player, passionate, self-motivated, insightful
- tagline for James by James: **WE MAKE IT HAPPEN!**

Your assessment of James:
- What is James known for?
- How do you believe James delivers value?
- How do you think James influences others?
- What would your tagline for James be?
- On a scale of 1 to 10—with 1 being "not really" and 10 being "absolutely"—how much would you enjoy working with James?

LEADER 3: TERRY

- sales associate with three years of experience
- with her company for one year
- a strong individual performer, producing results that have exceeded expectations
- known for reducing the typical sales cycle and closing deals
- focuses relentlessly on customers and their needs as part of her winning formula—not afraid to knock down obstacles along the way
- rumored to be under consideration to head her first sales team
- strengths (based on 360-degree feedback assessment): decisiveness, leading change, risk-taking, purposefulness, self-motivation, flexibility
- development needs (based on 360-degree feedback assessment): building collaborative relationships, forging cooperation, self-insight, sound judgment
- words others use to describe Terry: self-motivated, intelligent, uncaring, determined, inflexible
- Terry's self-description: competitive, self-motivated, innovative, leader
- tagline for Terry by Terry: **I MAKE IT HAPPEN!**

Your assessment of Terry:
- What is Terry known for?
- How do you believe Terry delivers value?
- How do you think Terry influences others?
- What would your tagline for Terry be?
- On a scale of 1 to 10—with 1 being "not really" and 10 being "absolutely"—how much would you enjoy working with Terry?

INSIGHTS FROM EXERCISE 1:

- How quickly were you able to complete your personal assessment of Parker, James, and Terry?
- How quickly do you think people judge you?
- Of the three leaders, which has the most effective leadership brand and why?
- Which has the least effective leadership brand and why?
- What could each of these three leaders do to improve his or her brand?
- Which has a brand most similar to your own current brand? Are you happy with the comparison?
- What do you take away from this exercise, and how has it helped you think about your brand?

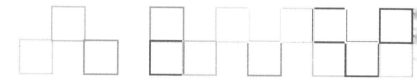

Exercise 2:
Bringing a Brand Perspective to Your Career

Now it is time to evaluate your own leadership brand and to determine what you are known for. Use the following questions as your guide:

- What is your current role, and how long have you been in it?
- How strong is your knowledge and skill level in this role?
- What would others say (or what have they said) about your knowledge and skill level? If you do not know, consider asking a few trusted colleagues and even your boss for some candid answers.
- What are you doing very well in your current role?
- What areas do you want to improve?
- Do those improvements involve knowledge, skills, or something else?
- Do you have any formal data from 360-degree feedback tools or personality assessments that can provide further insights on your strengths and areas that need development? If not, can you ask your organization to have you complete a formal assessment?
- What words would people use to describe you and why?
- What are your own descriptors for yourself and why?
- Are you satisfied with your ability to reach both your personal goals and career goals?
- What is your tagline for yourself?
- On a scale of 1 to 10—with 1 being "not satisfied at all" and 10 being "this is exactly what I want my brand to be"—what rating do you give yourself?

How to Define and
Cultivate an Aspirational Brand

Now that you have completed an analysis of your current leadership brand, what's next? How do you use what you've learned?

The most successful leaders continue to develop throughout their careers in order to reach their full potential. If you want to model that behavior, think about where you are today and where you would like to head in the future.

An authentic leadership brand will align with your sense of purpose, your values, and what matters to you most. It will reflect the roles you play, the work you spend the most time doing, how you interact with others, and the leadership contribution you consistently make.

You may find, though, that your current leadership brand isn't aligned with your values or with how you want to be known. In fact, your current brand may be limiting you as you search for new roles and opportunities. You may find yourself wanting people to know who you *really* are and what you are capable of.

If that's the case, defining and developing an aspirational brand grounded in your true values can help you move forward and reach your goals.

Grounding Your Aspirational Brand in Authenticity

Being authentic is about leading in a way that is natural for you and a reflection of your individual style and strengths. Feeling authentic and living a life strongly connected to your belief system can be energizing and can promote growth, learning, and psychological well-being.

If you try to be someone that you aren't, eventually others will see through your deception. Your inauthenticity can become a disruptive force in the organization as others talk about and try to anticipate what you might do next. You can even end up derailing your career.

How do you develop an aspirational brand that will reflect your innermost, authentic self? Before you make any changes, be sure to get a truthful picture of your current image. Take time to understand how others see you and why. Seek input from colleagues, your boss, and direct reports. Ask your friends, children, spouse, or significant other. Each of these points of view will provide insights into how your words and behaviors are viewed by the people around you.

Next, remind yourself that genuine change is rarely dramatic. Leaders making radical changes overnight are likely to be viewed with suspicion. Small, incremental changes that mesh with your values are more likely to be sustainable—and believed.

With that in mind, consider the gap between the image others have of you and the image you wish you were projecting. Decide what you could immediately begin working on and focus on one or two areas where small improvements could have the greatest benefit.

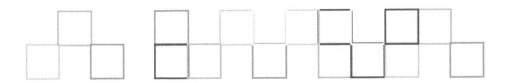

Techniques for Evolving Your Brand

Here are a few techniques you might try as you begin to evolve toward your aspirational leadership brand and change how you interact with others to help create direction, alignment, and commitment.

Tell stories. Give memorable examples that can engage others and interest them in what you are saying. Describe what happened, how a problem was solved, or how someone did something notable.

Master your message. Focus on clarity of thought and message and think carefully about what you want to say. Every question and conversation is an opportunity to share your ideas, vision, and values.

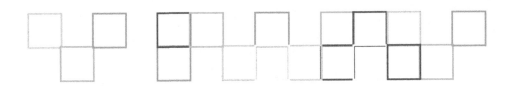

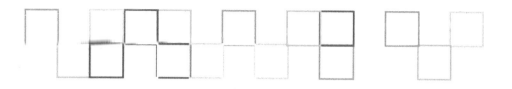

Focus on "we." Use inclusive language like "we" and "us" in order to inspire others and promote collaboration.

Smile. Tap into your personal warmth. Leaders who project a friendly image are typically perceived as more effective, engaging, and interesting.

Find a mentor, coach, and/or a trusted colleague. Solicit ideas on how you can address especially challenging issues and improve your leadership effectiveness and brand.

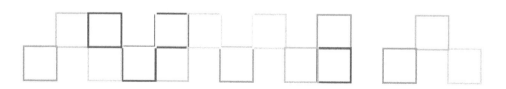

Exercise: Linking Your Brand to Your Values

The list of values below is derived from a set of values used in CCL leadership development programs. This tool helps us ensure the development goals of leaders participating in our programs align with the important values they seek to live and work by. These values can be useful as you evaluate how to link your aspirational brand to the things that matter most to you.

Achievement A sense of accomplishment, mastery.	**Change/Variety** Absence of routine. Work responsibilities, daily activities, or settings that change frequently. Unpredictability.	**Family** Time spent with spouse, children, parents, extended family, etc.	**Loyalty** Faithfulness. Duty. Dedication.
Activity High-pace conditions where work is done rapidly.	**Collaboration** Close, cooperative working relationships with group.	**Friendship** Close personal relationships with others.	**Order** Respectful of authority, rules, and regulations. A sense of stability, routine, predictability.
Advancement Growth, seniority, and promotion resulting from work well done.	**Community** To serve and support a purpose that supersedes personal desires. To make a difference.	**Happiness** Finding satisfaction, joy, or pleasure.	**Personal Development** Dedicated to maximizing one's potential.
Adventure New and challenging opportunities. Excitement. Risk.	**Competence** Demonstrating a high degree of proficiency and knowledge. Showing above-average effectiveness and efficiency at tasks.	**Help Others** Helping other people attain their goals. Providing care and support.	**Physical Fitness** Staying in shape through exercise and physical activity.
Aesthetics Appreciation of the beauty of things, ideas, surroundings, personal space, etc.	**Competition** Rivalry, with winning as the goal.	**Humor** The ability to laugh at oneself and life.	**Recognition** Positive feedback and public credit for work well done. Respect and admiration.

Affiliation
Interaction with people. Recognition as a member of a particular group. Involvement. Belonging.

Compassion
A deep awareness and sympathy for another's suffering.

Influence
Having an impact or effect on the attitudes or opinions of other people. The power of persuasion.

Reflection
Taking time out to think about the past, present, and future.

Affluence
High income, financial success, prosperity.

Courage
Willingness to stand up for one's beliefs.

Integrity
Acting in accord with moral and ethical standards. Honesty. Sincerity. Truth. Trustworthiness.

Responsibility
Dependability, reliability, accountability for results.

Authority
Position and the power to control events and activities of others.

Creativity
Discovering developing, or designing new ideas, programs, or things using innovation and imagination. Creating unique formats.

Justice
Fairness, equality, doing the "right" thing.

Self-respect
Pride, self-esteem, sense of personal identity.

Autonomy
Ability to act independently, with few constraints. Self-sufficiency.

Economic Security
Steady and secure employment. Adequate financial reward. Low risk.

Knowledge
The pursuit of understanding, skill, and expertise. Continuous learning.

Spirituality
Strong spiritual or religious beliefs. Moral fulfillment.

Status
Impressing or gaining respect of friends, family, and community by the nature and/or level of responsibility of one's job or by association with a prestigious group or organization.

Balance
Giving proper weight to each area of one's life.

Enjoyment
Fun, joy, and laughter.

Location
Choice of a place to live (town, geographic area, etc.) that is conducive to one's lifestyle

Challenge
Continually facing complex and demanding tasks and problems.

Fame
To become prominent, famous, well known.

Love
To be involved in close, affectionate relationships. Intimacy.

Wisdom
Sound judgement based on knowledge, experience, and understanding.

STEP 1: What do you stand for?

- Make a paper copy of the values chart. Cut out each label to create a set of 44. Sort the labels into the following categories:
    - Always Valued
    - Often Valued
    - Sometimes Valued
    - Seldom Valued
    - Rarely Valued
- Stand back and look at the results of your sort. Does anything surprise you?
- Five years ago, would you have categorized any of the values differently? If so, why?
- Examine the values you placed under "Always Valued." Which resonate with you most deeply and reflect the inner you?
- Which values do you want to aspire to develop over the next five years?

STEP 2: What outcomes do you hope to achieve?

Think about the stakeholders you have served over the last couple of years, both internal and external to your organization.

- Who were they?
- What did they want?
- What projects did you work on during this time?
  What did you find challenging?
- What aspects of these projects were the most enjoyable and why?
- What aspects do you think brought out the best in you and why?
- What unique skills, knowledge, attitudes, and behaviors did you bring to the work?
- What feedback did you receive directly or indirectly?

21

STEP 3: How does your work connect with your values?

Now let's connect the stories of your projects with the values you identified in Step 1. In what ways were your values at play in those projects? From feedback you received, what did others notice and value about your work and their interactions with you? As you reflect, are any values important to you missing from the list we provided? Are there any that you now would categorize differently?

STEP 4: What do you want to be known for?

Based on what you like to do and what you consider fun and challenging, what do you aspire to be known for in the future? What stakeholders will you serve? What needs do you hope to fulfill in a unique way? How well does this aspirational view of your brand match the values you cherish the most?

STEP 5: What is your unique contribution?

If you were to summarize the unique contribution you hope to bring to projects, what would your tagline be?

One way to craft your own tagline is to create a catchphrase and/or an image that illustrates the essence of your leadership brand. As you think about your tagline, consider what you stand for and what you deliver. Your tagline should also convey your spirit succinctly so others understand your meaning even if they have never met you. Find a symbol or an image that portrays the essence of your brand, and combine it with a catchphrase that best matches the promise you want your brand to make. Then, share the slogan with others and get feedback. Does it fit you? Does it need changes? Once you've finalized your tagline, post it prominently and publicly, where it can serve as a reminder to you and others of the brand you aspire to.

STEP 6: Creating your brand summary.

Now let's pull together the work you've done into a summary of your aspirational brand. Include the following:

- Your tagline.

    EXAMPLE: "To be an inspiration to young people everywhere by helping them identify their unique gifts and talents."

    EXAMPLE: "To help my clients unlock their inner athlete and accomplish things they didn't think were possible."

- The services you will uniquely deliver to your stakeholders.
- Your top values and how they will influence the way you deliver your services.
- Create a poster with your brand summary, and display it where you can see it every day to keep you focused on the future you want to create.

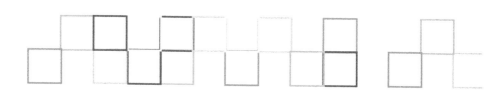

STEP 7: Designing an action plan.

To bring your aspirational brand to life, it is important to take actions that will move you in the right direction. Here are some strategic steps that can help:

- Develop any new competencies you may need. If you aren't yet where you want to be with your brand, you may need to focus on your leadership development plan. What new knowledge will you need to bring your aspirational brand to life, and how will you acquire it? What new skills, attitudes, and behaviors might you need to develop, and how will you develop them?
- Solicit help. Having an effective support network can be vital to your brand-building plan. Are there others you can approach for feedback and support, such as your boss or trusted colleagues?
- Assess your progress. Select a few key metrics to help you determine your progress in building your aspirational brand. Use metrics like the ones below to bring focus to the feedback you solicit about your work and to determine how effectively you are engaging with others in support of your shared direction, alignment, and commitment.
    - Do others come to you for your opinion?
    - Do others ask to work with you?
    - How often do others come to you with new opportunities or challenges?
    - Are you receiving feedback on things you are trying to do more of or less of?
    - How many times do you do something you've wanted to start doing?
    - Are you managing your time well, meeting deadlines, and accomplishing your goals?
    - Are you setting goals and working to achieve them?

How to Reinforce Your Personal Leadership Brand Online

Most of us head to the Internet to search for background on someone before we meet them. Recruiters and talent management executives typically do the same as they screen candidates for job openings or promotions. This means the first impression someone has of you and your brand is often what they find online.

In the early days of social media, many individuals attempted to separate their personal and professional activity online. However, any web search will turn up both. It is better to think holistically and to acknowledge that all the online posts you make, whether personal or professional, can enhance or detract from your leadership brand. They paint a story about you and represent your expertise, experience, points of view, and reputation.

Audit your online brand.

If someone were to conduct an online search for background on you right now, what information would show up? It's time to conduct your own search and find out. Are there any surprises? What do you like about the information you see? What would you like to change?

Online Brand Building: Tips and Considerations

With a bit of thoughtful reflection, you can begin to build an online presence that supports the leadership brand you want to cultivate. Here are some tips and considerations to get you started.

Look for examples. Identify professionals with online brands you admire. What do you notice? How have they articulated their value? Where do they appear online, and how does the location enhance their brand?

Focus on what matters to you. Think about your own leadership brand and the values, expertise, and points of view you want to be known for. How can you support your brand online? What topics do you want to be associated with, and where do you want to show up?

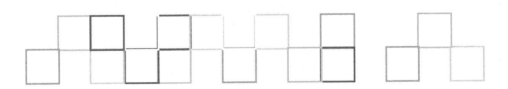

Get social. One of the easiest and most powerful ways to cultivate your leadership brand online is through social media. Popular professional networks like LinkedIn, for example, can be a great place to start. They offer an easy way to stay connected to others in your field. You also might contribute to blogs and newsletters published by your company or those sponsored by professional associations. You can even create your own website or blog spot that will reflect the essence of the brand image you want to project.

Speak up. Consider posting comments about articles, presentations or events that have influenced you. Create original digital content that expresses your interests and reinforces your brand. You might join a LinkedIn community of interest and share tips and ideas that establish you as a thought leader in your field. You might use your Facebook page to comment on news articles related to what you do or to talk about what you learned at a recent conference. Remember that clarity and consistency of message are fundamental. If the information and opinions you share lack focus, you could actually erode your brand by not making it clear what you are interested in and stand for.

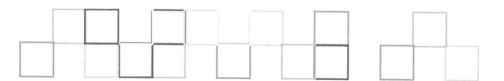

Evolving Your Leadership Brand throughout Your Career

Leadership brand goes well beyond superficial image and how you look, sound, or speak. It instead involves unlocking those personal qualities that impact how you interact with others to achieve shared alignment, direction, and commitment.

As your career evolves, so should your brand. In fact, the leadership brand you cultivated as a newly minted manager will likely be significantly different than the leadership brand you will have as a senior executive.

You may want to revisit some of the insights you've gained from the exercises in this book and review your brand once a year or during important career transition points (e.g., a promotion or special assignment). Continue to ask yourself these questions:

What do I value, and do my values still reflect who I am?

For most of us, what we value shifts due to maturity and life experiences. A shift in values often fuels profound life changes, which in turn drive us to behave differently. That changing behavior ultimately impacts our leadership brand. It's worth checking in with yourself periodically to understand how your values might have shifted over time.

What am I known for?

How do I want to be known? Each time we interact with others, both professionally and personally, we develop a reputation. Periodically check your reputation—either formally through 360-degree assessment and regular performance reviews—or informally through feedback from trusted peers and mentors. Are you coming across the way you intended? What might you fine-tune? What are you doing well that you should keep doing?

Am I doing everything I can to build my brand beyond the workplace?

Often, the best career opportunities come when we proactively promote our ideas and work. Periodically, check to see if your digital brand reflects the brand you want to cultivate. Do the ideas and images you share online still reflect who you are? Are you missing opportunities to be known in other categories or industries that could potentially enhance your brand?

Remember, the way you engage in the social process of leadership to help your team achieve shared alignment, direction, and commitment forms the basis of your brand—impacting what people will say about you when you aren't in the room.

When you consciously and authentically build your leadership brand and then effectively communicate it, you help people understand the value you bring to your work and create opportunities for your own personal growth and leadership influence throughout your career.

29

BACKGROUND

The idea for a book on leadership brand grew out of our experiences working with students in CCL's *Leadership Fundamentals* course. We found many of the entry-level managers attending shared a common plight. They hoped to move up in their organization, but they felt no one knew who they were or what they were capable of. They had discovered that their own good works simply weren't enough.

We came to suspect the same dilemma applies to individuals across most any organization. They have aspirations but don't know how to build their reputation and have their name bubble up in the right places. We've become passionate about helping these individuals step out from the shadows and exercise their full potential by building and leveraging their leadership brand.

SUGGESTED RESOURCES

Bunker, K., & Wakefield, M. (2005). *Leading with authenticity in times of transition.* Greensboro, NC: Center for Creative Leadership.

Cartwright, T. (2009). *Changing yourself and your reputation.* Greensboro, NC: Center for Creative Leadership.

Criswell, C., & Campbell, D. (2008). *Building an authentic leadership image.* Greensboro, NC: Center for Creative Leadership.

Evans, C. (2015). *Leadership trust: Build it, keep it.* Greensboro, NC: Center for Creative Leadership.

Hannum, K. (2007). *Social identity: Knowing yourself, leading others.* Greensboro, NC: Center for Creative Leadership.

Hernez-Broome, G., & McLaughlin, C. (2007). *Selling yourself without selling out: A leader's guide to ethical self-promotion.* Greensboro, NC: Center for Creative Leadership.

McCauley, C., & Fick-Cooper, L. (2015). *Direction, alignment, commitment: Achieving better results through leadership.* Greensboro, NC: Center for Creative Leadership.

Palus, C. J., & Horth, D. M. (2014). *Leadership metaphor explorer.* Greensboro, NC: Center for Creative Leadership.

Palus, C. J., & Horth, D. M. (2014). *Visual explorer.* Greensboro, NC: Center for Creative Leadership.

Sternbergh, B., & Weitzel, S. R. (2007). *Setting your development goals: Start with your values.* Greensboro, NC: Center for Creative Leadership.

ABOUT THE CENTER FOR CREATIVE LEADERSHIP

The Center for Creative Leadership (CCL) is a top-ranked, global provider of leadership development. By leveraging the power of leadership to drive results that matter most to clients, CCL transforms individual leaders, teams, organizations, and society. Our array of cutting-edge solutions is steeped in extensive research and experience gained from working with hundreds of thousands of leaders at all levels. Ranked among the world's Top 5 providers of executive education by *Financial Times* and in the Top 10 by *Bloomberg BusinessWeek*, CCL has offices in Greensboro, NC; Colorado Springs, CO; San Diego, CA; Brussels, Belgium; Moscow, Russia; Addis Ababa, Ethiopia; Johannesburg, South Africa; Singapore; Gurgaon, India; and Shanghai, China.

Center for
Creative
Leadership·

IDEAS
INTO
ACTION

ORDERING INFORMATION

To get more information, to order other books in the Ideas Into Action Series, or to find out about bulk-order discounts, please contact us by phone at 336-545-2810 or visit our online bookstore at www.ccl.org/books.

Center for
Creative
Leadership®

Keep the learning
going by tapping
into CCL's **digital
development
solutions,** which
provide **anytime**
access to world-class
tools and resources.

- Customized Blended Solutions
- In-House Solutions
- Lead 2.0
- Self-paced eCourses
- Digital Guidebook Library
- Webinars

CCL's array of digital learning products helps you build
leadership excellence when and where you need it most.
Learn more at **www.ccl.org/digitallearning.**

CPSIA information can be obtained
at www.ICGtesting.com
Printed in the USA
BVOW05s0157120117
473156BV00005B/9/P